★★★★★
MLB TEAMS

San Diego PADRES

KENNY ABDO

Fly!
An Imprint of Abdo Zoom
abdobooks.com

abdobooks.com

Published by Abdo Zoom, a division of ABDO, P.O. Box 398166, Minneapolis, Minnesota 55439.

Printed in the United States of America, North Mankato, Minnesota.
102025
012026

Photo Credits: Alamy, AP Images, Getty Images, Shutterstock
Production Contributors: Kenny Abdo, Jennie Forsberg, Grace Hansen
Design Contributors: Candice Keimig, Neil Klinepier

Library of Congress Control Number: 2025936812

Publisher's Cataloging-in-Publication Data

Names: Abdo, Kenny, author.
Title: San Diego Padres / by Kenny Abdo
Description: Minneapolis, Minnesota : Abdo Zoom, 2026 | Series: MLB teams | Includes online resources and index.
Identifiers: ISBN 9798384940302 (lib. bdg.) | ISBN 9798384941064 (ebook) | ISBN 9798384941446 (read-to-me ebook)
Subjects: LCSH: San Diego Padres (Baseball team)--Juvenile literature. | Baseball teams--Juvenile literature. | Professional sports--Juvenile literature. | Sports franchises--Juvenile literature. | Major League Baseball (Organization)--Juvenile literature.
Classification: DDC 796.357--dc23

Table of CONTENTS

PADRES

Since 1969, the Padres have brought big swings and sunny days to San Diego!

DIEGO
13

From early struggles to big October runs, the Padres have proven that every team gets its shot at glory, even if the road there is longer than the coast of California.

SD
PADRES
Rawlings

BATTER UP!

The San Diego Padres began playing in Major League Baseball (MLB) in 1969. They joined the **National League (NL)** as one of four new teams that year. The early seasons were tough, with many losses and few standout players.

In the 1970s, the Padres began to show promise. Dave Winfield joined the team in 1973 and became a star outfielder. In 1976, Randy Jones won the **Cy Young Award** with 22 wins and a 2.74 **ERA**. In 1978, the Padres nabbed their first winning season!

In 1984, the Padres reached the playoffs for the first time. Led by Tony Gwynn and Goose Gossage, the team took home the **NL pennant**. Though the Padres lost the World Series to the Tigers, it was a successful season!

GRAND SLAMS

The Padres had some major shake-ups in the 1990s. New ownership, big trades, and rising stars helped get the team into the 1996 playoffs. The Padres had another great year in 1998. Trevor Hoffman saved 53 games leading the team to win the **NL** title! However, the Padres lost the World Series to the Yankees.

SD
PADRES

The Padres had a strong run in the mid-2000s. The team captured the **NL** West title and reached the playoffs in 2005 and 2006!

In 2007, Jake Peavy led the charge by winning the **Cy Young Award** with 19 wins and a 2.54 **ERA**.

The 2010s took the Padres on a wild ride of wins and losses. The team changed up the roster by adding young stars such as Manny Machado and Fernando Tatis Jr. In 2019, Tatis hit 22 home runs in just 84 games. That year, the Padres set a new team **record** for home runs in a season!

PADRES

MACHADO
13
PROFAR

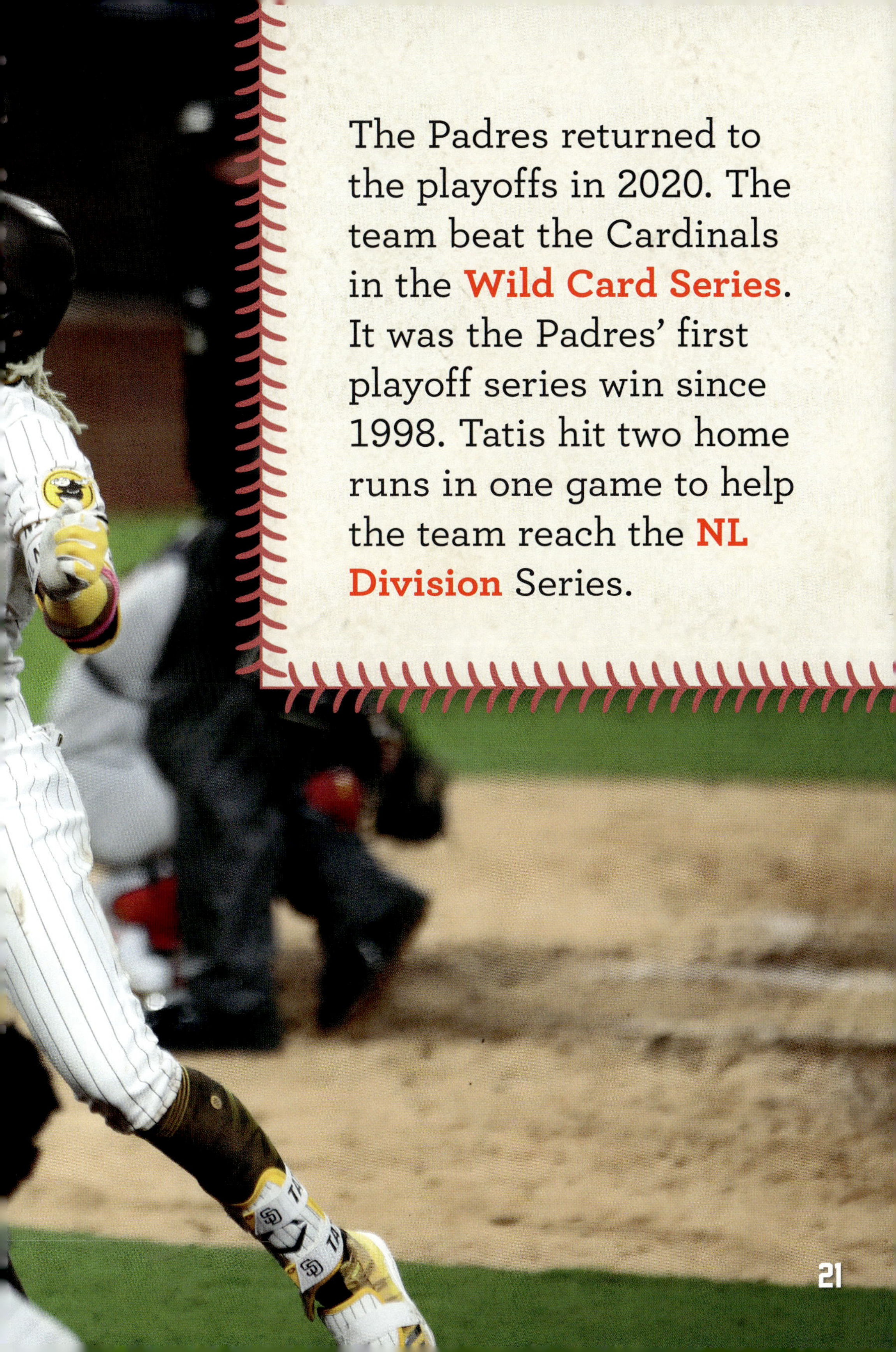

The Padres returned to the playoffs in 2020. The team beat the Cardinals in the **Wild Card Series**. It was the Padres' first playoff series win since 1998. Tatis hit two home runs in one game to help the team reach the **NL Division** Series.

The Padres reached the 2022 **NL** Championship Series after winning 89 games in the regular season. However, they lost to the Phillies after five tough games.

The team struggled in 2025 despite a 90–72 regular season **record** and making it to the playoffs. Their run ended quickly, but fans in San Diego hope the long wait for a championship is close to ending.

HALL OF FAME

Tony Gwynn was one of the best hitters in baseball history. He collected more than 3,000 hits and won eight batting titles, all with the Padres. Gwynn struck out only 434 times in his 20 seasons with the team. He was **inducted** into the Baseball Hall of Fame in 2007.

31

Dave Winfield was a star outfielder for the Padres. He hit home runs, stole bases, and drove in almost 600 runs with the team. Winfield made four **All-Star** teams. In 1979, he hit 34 home runs and had 118 **RBIs**, his best season in San Diego. Winfield was named to the Baseball Hall of Fame in 2001.

Trevor Hoffman was one of the greatest closers in baseball. He saved 552 games with the Padres and struck out more than 1,000 batters. In 1998, Hoffman helped the team get to the World Series. He was entered into the Baseball Hall of Fame in 2018.

GLOSSARY

All-Star – a team consisting of athletes chosen as the best at their positions from all teams in a league or region.

Cy Young Award – an annual American baseball award given to the best pitcher in each of the two MLB leagues.

division – a number of teams grouped together in a sport for competitive purposes.

Earned-Run Average (ERA) – the average number of earned runs per game scored against a pitcher.

inducted – brought in as a member.

National League (NL) – one of two 15-team leagues that make up MLB.

pennant – the title achieved by the team that wins its division or league championship.

record – a top achievement by a team or player that no one has done before; a team's season total of wins and losses.

Runs Batted In (RBI) – a statistic that credits a batter for making a play that allows a run to be scored.

Wild Card Series – the first round of the postseason.

ONLINE RESOURCES

To learn more about the San Diego Padres, please visit **abdobooklinks.com** or scan this QR code. These links are routinely monitored and updated to provide the most current information available.

INDEX